I0011345

Dr Muggles' mind relaxer

Steven Johnson

Dr Muggles' mind relaxer

ISBN: 10: 1505872693
ISBN-13: 978-1505872699

CONTENTS

1 CLEAR THE CLUTTER

So you have forgotten one of your internet passwords. Good job it wasn't your internet banking password. You searched the house for that scrap of paper where you had a few passwords written down but didn't find it right?

Or worst still you entered a password for that website you don't go to often, but now they have 50% off *all purchases*, and *free shipping*, but your password was incorrect. You knew it was the right one, but hang on maybe it started with a capital letter or maybe it had this month's date as part of it, or your pet's name (but hang on Bugsy died last year) or maybe the password you were entering was the one you use for that woodturning craft site you like, or your favorite recipe site. Aaagh! I can't even remember my eBay log in any more.

Relax! Take a few deep breaths. Remember in the olden days, when, according to your grandparents they used to write everything down? They did it for a reason. So that they didn't have to carry all that clutter, all those little bits of information filed away in neat filing cabinets in the mind until the day came when they had to remember something important.

Perhaps if you could keep all your passwords in one place you wouldn't have to try and remember them all the time. Stop wasting your brains processing power on remembering all of your log-in passwords and use Dr Muggle's mind relaxer. A simple password manager cleverly disguised as one of those self-help books you keep meaning to read one day.

I hope this book helps you to clear the clutter of your mind.

2 FAMILY AND CONTACTS

Family member or Contact _____

Web address _____

Log-in or username _____

Password_____

Notes _____

_____

Family member or Contact _____

Web address _____

Log-in or username _____

Password_____

Notes _____

_____

Family member or Contact _____

Web address _____

Log-in or username _____

Password_____

Notes _____

_____

Family member or Contact _____

Web address _____

Log-in or username _____

Password_____

Notes _____

_____

Family member or Contact _____

Web address _____

Log-in or username _____

Password_____

Notes _____

_____

Family member or Contact _____

Web address _____

Log-in or username _____

Password_____

Notes _____

_____

Family member or Contact _____

Web address _____

Log-in or username _____

Password_____

Notes _____

_____

Family member or Contact _____

Web address _____

Log-in or username _____

Password_____

Notes _____

_____

Family member or Contact _____

Web address _____

Log-in or username _____

Password_____

Notes _____

_____

Family member or Contact _____

Web address _____

Log-in or username _____

Password_____

Notes _____

_____

Family member or Contact _____

Web address _____

Log-in or username _____

Password_____

Notes _____

_____

Family member or Contact _____

Web address _____

Log-in or username _____

Password_____

Notes _____

_____

Family member or Contact _____

Web address _____

Log-in or username _____

Password_____

Notes _____

_____

Family member or Contact _____

Web address _____

Log-in or username _____

Password_____

Notes _____

_____

Family member or Contact _____

Web address _____

Log-in or username _____

Password_____

Notes _____

_____

Family member or Contact _____

Web address _____

Log-in or username _____

Password_____

Notes _____

_____

Family member or Contact _____

Web address _____

Log-in or username _____

Password_____

Notes _____

_____

Family member or Contact _____

Web address _____

Log-in or username _____

Password_____

Notes _____

_____

3 BANKING AND IMPORTANT STUFF

Bank or Institution_____

Account_____

Web address _____

Log-in or username _____

Password_____

Notes _____

Bank or Institution_____

Account_____

Web address _____

Log-in or username _____

Password_____

Notes _____

Bank or Institution_____

Account_____

Web address _____

Log-in or username _____

Password_____

Notes _____

Bank or Institution_____

Account_____

Web address _____

Log-in or username _____

Password_____

Notes _____

Bank or Institution_____

Account_____

Web address _____

Log-in or username _____

Password_____

Notes _____

Bank or Institution_____

Account_____

Web address _____

Log-in or username _____

Password_____

Notes _____

Bank or Institution_____

Account_____

Web address _____

Log-in or username _____

Password_____

Notes _____

Bank or Institution_____

Account_____

Web address _____

Log-in or username _____

Password_____

Notes _____

Bank or Institution_____

Account_____

Web address _____

Log-in or username _____

Password_____

Notes _____

Bank or Institution_____

Account_____

Web address _____

Log-in or username _____

Password_____

Notes _____

Bank or Institution_____

Account_____

Web address _____

Log-in or username _____

Password_____

Notes _____

Bank or Institution_____

Account_____

Web address _____

Log-in or username _____

Password_____

Notes _____

Bank or Institution_____

Account_____

Web address _____

Log-in or username _____

Password_____

Notes _____

Bank or Institution_____

Account_____

Web address _____

Log-in or username _____

Password_____

Notes _____

Bank or Institution_____

Account_____

Web address _____

Log-in or username _____

Password_____

Notes _____

Bank or Institution_____

Account_____

Web address _____

Log-in or username _____

Password_____

Notes _____

Bank or Institution_____

Account_____

Web address _____

Log-in or username _____

Password_____

Notes _____

Bank or Institution_____

Account_____

Web address _____

Log-in or username _____

Password_____

Notes _____

Bank or Institution_____

Account_____

Web address _____

Log-in or username _____

Password_____

Notes _____

Bank or Institution_____

Account_____

Web address _____

Log-in or username _____

Password_____

Notes _____

Bank or Institution_____

Account_____

Web address _____

Log-in or username _____

Password_____

Notes _____

Bank or Institution_____

Account_____

Web address _____

Log-in or username _____

Password_____

Notes _____

Bank or Institution_____

Account_____

Web address _____

Log-in or username _____

Password_____

Notes _____

Bank or Institution_____

Account_____

Web address _____

Log-in or username _____

Password_____

Notes _____

4 SHOP 'TILL YOU DROP

Shopping site_____

Web address _____

Log-in or username _____

Password_____

Notes _____

_____

Shopping Site_____

Web address _____

Log-in or username _____

Password_____

Notes _____

_____

Shopping Site_____

Web address _____

Log-in or username _____

Password_____

Notes _____

_____

Shopping site_____

Web address _____

Log-in or username _____

Password_____

Notes _____

_____

Shopping Site_____

Web address _____

Log-in or username _____

Password_____

Notes _____

_____

Shopping Site_____

Web address _____

Log-in or username _____

Password_____

Notes _____

_____

Shopping site_____

Web address _____

Log-in or username _____

Password_____

Notes _____

_____

Shopping Site_____

Web address _____

Log-in or username _____

Password_____

Notes _____

_____

Shopping Site_____

Web address _____

Log-in or username _____

Password_____

Notes _____

_____

Shopping site_____

Web address _____

Log-in or username _____

Password_____

Notes _____

_____

Shopping Site_____

Web address _____

Log-in or username _____

Password_____

Notes _____

_____

Shopping Site_____

Web address _____

Log-in or username _____

Password_____

Notes _____

_____

Shopping site_____

Web address _____

Log-in or username _____

Password_____

Notes _____

_____

Shopping Site_____

Web address _____

Log-in or username _____

Password_____

Notes _____

_____

Shopping Site_____

Web address _____

Log-in or username _____

Password_____

Notes _____

_____

Shopping site_____

Web address _____

Log-in or username _____

Password_____

Notes _____

_____

Shopping Site_____

Web address _____

Log-in or username _____

Password_____

Notes _____

_____

Shopping Site_____

Web address _____

Log-in or username _____

Password_____

Notes _____

_____

21

Shopping site_____

Web address _____

Log-in or username _____

Password_____

Notes _____

_____

Shopping Site_____

Web address _____

Log-in or username _____

Password_____

Notes _____

_____

Shopping Site_____

Web address _____

Log-in or username _____

Password_____

Notes _____

_____

Shopping site_____

Web address _____

Log-in or username _____

Password_____

Notes _____

_____

Shopping Site_____

Web address _____

Log-in or username _____

Password_____

Notes _____

_____

Shopping Site_____

Web address _____

Log-in or username _____

Password_____

Notes _____

_____

Shopping site_____

Web address _____

Log-in or username _____

Password_____

Notes _____

_____

Shopping Site_____

Web address _____

Log-in or username _____

Password_____

Notes _____

_____

Shopping Site_____

Web address _____

Log-in or username _____

Password_____

Notes _____

_____

5 ENTERTAINMENT

Entertainment site_____

Web address _____

Log-in or username _____

Password_____

Notes _____

_____

Entertainment site_____

Web address _____

Log-in or username _____

Password_____

Notes _____

_____

Entertainment Site_____

Web address _____

Log-in or username _____

Password_____

Notes _____

_____

Entertainment site_____

Web address _____

Log-in or username _____

Password_____

Notes _____

_____

Entertainment site_____

Web address _____

Log-in or username _____

Password_____

Notes _____

_____

Entertainment Site_____

Web address _____

Log-in or username _____

Password_____

Notes _____

_____

Entertainment site_____

Web address _____

Log-in or username _____

Password_____

Notes _____

_____

Entertainment site_____

Web address _____

Log-in or username _____

Password_____

Notes _____

_____

Entertainment Site_____

Web address _____

Log-in or username _____

Password_____

Notes _____

_____

Entertainment site_____

Web address _____

Log-in or username _____

Password_____

Notes _____

_____

Entertainment site_____

Web address _____

Log-in or username _____

Password_____

Notes _____

_____

Entertainment Site_____

Web address _____

Log-in or username _____

Password_____

Notes _____

_____

Entertainment site_____

Web address _____

Log-in or username _____

Password_____

Notes _____

_____

Entertainment site_____

Web address _____

Log-in or username _____

Password_____

Notes _____

_____

Entertainment Site_____

Web address _____

Log-in or username _____

Password_____

Notes _____

_____

Entertainment site_____

Web address _____

Log-in or username _____

Password_____

Notes _____

_____

Entertainment site_____

Web address _____

Log-in or username _____

Password_____

Notes _____

_____

Entertainment Site_____

Web address _____

Log-in or username _____

Password_____

Notes _____

_____

Entertainment site_____

Web address _____

Log-in or username _____

Password_____

Notes _____

_____

Entertainment site_____

Web address _____

Log-in or username _____

Password_____

Notes _____

_____

Entertainment Site_____

Web address _____

Log-in or username _____

Password_____

Notes _____

_____

Entertainment site_____

Web address _____

Log-in or username _____

Password_____

Notes _____

_____

Entertainment site_____

Web address _____

Log-in or username _____

Password_____

Notes _____

_____

Entertainment Site_____

Web address _____

Log-in or username _____

Password_____

Notes _____

_____

Entertainment site_____

Web address _____

Log-in or username _____

Password_____

Notes _____

_____

Entertainment site_____

Web address _____

Log-in or username _____

Password_____

Notes _____

_____

Entertainment Site_____

Web address _____

Log-in or username _____

Password_____

Notes _____

_____

Entertainment site_____

Web address _____

Log-in or username _____

Password_____

Notes _____

_____

Entertainment site_____

Web address _____

Log-in or username _____

Password_____

Notes _____

_____

Entertainment Site_____

Web address _____

Log-in or username _____

Password_____

Notes _____

_____

6 OTHER INTEREST WEB SITES

Web site of interest_____

Web address _____

Log-in or username _____

Password_____

Notes _____

_____

Web site of interest_____

Web address _____

Log-in or username _____

Password_____

Notes _____

_____

Web site of interest_____

Web address _____

Log-in or username _____

Password_____

Notes _____

_____

Web site of interest_____

Web address _____

Log-in or username _____

Password_____

Notes _____

_____

Web site of interest_____

Web address _____

Log-in or username _____

Password_____

Notes _____

_____

Web site of interest_____

Web address _____

Log-in or username _____

Password_____

Notes _____

_____

Web site of interest_____

Web address _____

Log-in or username _____

Password_____

Notes _____

_____

Web site of interest_____

Web address _____

Log-in or username _____

Password_____

Notes _____

_____

Web site of interest_____

Web address _____

Log-in or username _____

Password_____

Notes _____

_____

Web site of interest_____

Web address _____

Log-in or username _____

Password_____

Notes _____

_____

Web site of interest_____

Web address _____

Log-in or username _____

Password_____

Notes _____

_____

Web site of interest_____

Web address _____

Log-in or username _____

Password_____

Notes _____

_____

Web site of interest_____

Web address _____

Log-in or username _____

Password_____

Notes _____

_____

Web site of interest_____

Web address _____

Log-in or username _____

Password_____

Notes _____

_____

Web site of interest_____

Web address _____

Log-in or username _____

Password_____

Notes _____

_____

Web site of interest_____

Web address _____

Log-in or username _____

Password_____

Notes _____

_____

Web site of interest_____

Web address _____

Log-in or username _____

Password_____

Notes _____

_____

Web site of interest_____

Web address _____

Log-in or username _____

Password_____

Notes _____

_____

Web site of interest_____

Web address _____

Log-in or username _____

Password_____

Notes _____

_____

Web site of interest_____

Web address _____

Log-in or username _____

Password_____

Notes _____

_____

Web site of interest_____

Web address _____

Log-in or username _____

Password_____

Notes _____

_____

7 OTHER STUFF YOU NEED TO RECORD

_____

_____

_____

_____

_____

_____

_____

_____

_____

_____

_____

_____

_____

_____

_____

_____

_____

_____

_____

_____

_____

_____

_____

www.ingramcontent.com/pod-product-compliance
Lightning Source LLC
Chambersburg PA
CBHW071033050326
40689CB00014B/3641